Edition THILL ltd Brussels

Brussels was founded in 580 by Saint Géry, the Bishop of Cambrai. According to the legend, he risked his life to cross the Forest of Soignes, and built a humble chapel on a small island in the Senne. A century later, that little island had become an important village, called «Broeksele». The town only developed in the XIth century. The first ramparts were built around 1100. In the XIIthe century, the town had become one of the staging points of the road between Bruges and Cologne. It kept on growing and spread outside its first walls in the XIIIth century. The present boulevards delimit the new town that was created. It prospered under the Dukes of Burgundy and Philip the Good lived there. The luxury crafts, the tapestries, the goldsmith's crafts flourished at the time. It remained very important under the Habsbourgs. During the reign of Philipp II, the seat of the central governement of the Netherlands was permanently established in Brussels. It was not long before the Spanish governors who were sent there roused the population's indignation. In 1695, during the wars of Louis XIV, Brussels was destroyed by the Marshal of Villeroy. The Market Place, the Town Hall and 4,000 houses were set on fire. Richard of Lorraine, brother-in-law of Queen Marie-Thérèse (1744-1780) brought the town some peace. Under the French Republic, it became the chief town of the Dyle department. Between 1815 and 1830, it alternated with La Haye the residence of the Kings of the Netherlands. The revolution which was to bring independence to the country started on August 24, 1830, during the night. King Leopold I made his solemn entrance on July 21, 1831. The transformation of Brussels began in the XVIIIth century and went on so that the suburbs increased and new districts were created at the end of the XIXth century and the beginning of the XXth century.

The Market Place is in the center of the old town; it is in the form of a rectangle (110m long and 68m wide) and is dominated by the Town Hall with its elegant belbry, which stands in front of the House of the King, and surrounded by ancient guildhouses of the XVIIth century. In the daytime, the flower market is held there, and in the evening the illuminated Market Place is a marvellous decor.

The **Town Hall** is the most remarkable ancient monument of Brussels and one of the most beautiful examples of Gothic architecture in Belgium. The left wing was built by the architect Jacques Van Thienen and dates from 1402; the right wing was built by an unknown architect in 1444. The Belfry is a masterpiece of elegance and lightness. It was built in 1449 by Jean Van Ruysbroeck. It is 90m high and is topped by a 5m high weathervane, representing Saint Michael downing the dragon. A porch of 17 arches stands along the first floor; the high casement-windows of the other two floors are decorated with sculptures and statues. A wide vaulted door gives access to the tower; statues adorn the arches and the tympanum of the rib. The abutments represent justice, prudence, peace, law, moderation and strength. In the inner court, two ponds decorated with allegirical statues represent two rivers: the Meuse and the Scheldt.

The **Hall of the City Council** is the former Hall of the States of Brabant. It is decorated with beautiful Brussels tapestries woven in the XVIIIth century by Leyniers and Reydams, from the designs of Janssens.

The **Maximilien Room** is adorned with tapestries telling the story of Clovis-life. They were woven in Brussels, from the designs of Charles Le Brun.

BRAS DE LA SENNE RUE ST GÉRY.
ET MOULIN DIT RUYSCHMOLEN

The **Anti-room of the Burgomaster** is entirely decorated with paintings by J.B. Van Moer, depicting old sites of the city which do not exist any more.

The **Wedding Room** was formerly used as a courtroom and as e meeting room for the representative of the nations. A mural embroidery on silk represents love and law, surmounted by a group of children symbolizing the hopes of wedding.

The **Gothic Room** is 25m long and 12m wide; it was used for important receptions and official ceremonies. It is decorated with sculptures, Gothic paneling and eight tapestries representing guilds, woven between 1875 and 1881, from the designs of G. Geets.

The **Grand Staircase** was decorated in the XIXth century and glorifies the communal power. The hall is flanked by statues of the Burgomasters.

The house of «**La Louve**» the guild of the archers. It is decorated with statues and sculptures. Marc De Vos sculpted the four statues on the second floor: truth, untruth, discord and peace. The gable is surmounted by a gilt phoenix.

«**Le Renard**» was the guild-house of the haber-dashers; it was built by Van Nerum and Marc De Vos.

«**Le Cornet**» also called the boatmen's house, was built in 1698 by Antoine Pastorana. The architect designed the gable in the shape of a poop to remind us of the house's purpose.

The house «**Le Sac**» was built in 1644 for the cabinet-makers and the coopers. The architect Markaert gave the gable the shape of a cupboard to honor the guild. Above the door, a significant sign: a man holds a bag into which another man drives.

«**La Brouette**» was erected in 1697 by the tanners'guild. The gable is decorated with garlands of flowers and fruit. In the niche stands the statue of Saint Giles, the patron saint of tanners.

«**La Maison des Boulangers**» or «**Roi d'Espagne**» was built by the guilt of the bakers. This was one of the most important and richest in the town. Above the entrance door is a gilt bust of the Bishop Saint Aubert, the patron Saint of bakers. In the middle of the third floor, a trophy frames the bust of Charles II, King of Spain. The house is topped by a octagonal dome surmounted by a Renomée with banderole.

The two following groups of houses are simpler but maintain the distinguishing features of old Brussels houses. Their original names are very interesting. The house **«L'Ane»** and **«Sainte Barbe»** show the same typical simplicity.

«Le Chêne» and «Le Petit Renard» were built under the same roof. These are simple buildings, with dormer windows on the roof as their only adornment.

The façade of «Le Paon» is decorated with gilt garlands. Its gable is characteristic of XVIIIth century houses.

«Le Heaume» has a very elegant façade.

The original wooden construction of « **La Maison du Roi** » dates back to the XIIIth century. This house was used as a store by the bakers. During the following centuries, it was altered and damaged several times. It became a temporary State jailhouse. The earls of Egmont and of Horn spent their last night in it, before being executed on June 5, 1568, on the Market Place. An inscription on the bases of the columns recalls the execution of the Belgian lords. The Duke of Brabant made a tax office of it, and it was then called the Ducal House. After the French had conquered Belgium, the house was declared Public House. The foreign governors exercising certain royal functions there wrongly called it the « House of the King ». But, in spite of its name, no King lived there. Between 1873 and 1895, the edifice was rebuilt in Gotic style by Victor Jamaer, from original plans. It is decorated with florid sculptures which are typical of his style. The central arch on the first floor is topped by two statues, of Mary of Burgundy who gave the House of the King to the city in 1417, and of her grandson Charles V, under whose reign the house was rebuilt.

The **House of the King** shelters the City Museum of Brussels. The museum contains a marvellous collection of Brussels earthenware and porcelain, collections which refer to the past of the city and the gallery of Manneken-Pis costumes.

- Pan, made by J. Artoisnete (XVIIIth century), decorated with green copper butterflies and caterpillars.

- Tulip tress, manufacture of Etterbeek (1787-1803).

- Teapot and cup, by J.A. Neeles (1798-1822).

- Plate, St Michael decor, made by C. Mombaers and D. Witsemberg (1705-1709).

- Cabbage-shaped Soup-tureen, green copper decoration by J. Artoisenet (XVIIIth century).

The façade of «**La Chambrette de l'Amman**» is decorated with the armorial bearings of Brabant and is therefore nowadays called «Aux Armes de Brabant».

«**Le Pigeon**» was the house of the painters. Victor Hugo lived there in 1852.

«**La Taupe**» and «**La Chaloupe d'Or**» belonged to the tailors'guild. Above the entrance door stands a bust of Sainte-Barbe, the patron Saint of tailors, and above the house, Saint Boniface in a blessing attitude.

In the XVth century, **«L'Ange»** belonged to the Abbey of Forest. It is built in a very harmonious Flemisch baroque style.

«Joseph et Anne» and **«Le Cerf»** are simple bourgeois houses.

«La Maison des Ducs de Brabant» includes a range of different houses: «La Bourse», «La Colline», «Pot d'Etain», «Moulin à Vent», «La Fortune» and «L'Ermitage». These houses belonged respectively to the tanners, the millers, the carpenters, the sculptors and the slate-quarry workers. The building was given that name because of the busts on the pilasters. This group of houses is one of the most imposing on the Market Place. The edifice looks like a great Italian palace but the engineer and controller of the public works, Guillaume de Bruyn, who drew the plans for the reconstruction, drew his inspiration from the principles of classical architecture. In the decoration of the façade, he maintained the Flemish tradition. The architect Dewez renoved a balustrade decorated with vases and decorated the tympanum of the façade with an allegory representing abundance.

«Le Mont Thabor» was a bourgeois house.
«La Rose» belonged to the family Van der Rosen in the XVth century. The façade is simple and well-proportioned.
Above «L'Arbre d'Or» or «Maison des Brasseurs» stands the equestrian statue of Charles of Lorraine. The brewery museum was laid out in the cellars XVIIth century.
«Le Cygne» was the house of the butcher's guild. It is topped by tree statues representing abundance, agriculture and the butcher's trade.
«L'Etoile» is one of the oldest houses on the place. Under the porch of the house, you can admire the statue of Everard 't Serclaes, the hero of the struggle between the guilds and the patricians in the XIVth century.

The annual procession of the «**Ommegang**» refers to a historical event: the feast the magistrate of Brussels organized on June 2, 1549, in honor of the Emperor Charles V, his son Philip and his sisters Eleonore, Queen of France, and Mary, Queen of Hungary.

The «**Musée des Costumes et Dentelles**» houses a collection of chasubles and richly embroidered ecclesiastical habits of the XVIIIth century; Brussels lace of the XVIth and XIXth centuries; civil dresses and costumes; documents dealing with the textile industry of the capital and a workshop of passementerie.

- Passementerie workshop dating from the XIXth century: loom, spinning wheel with spools, spooling frame with spindles, and wheel used to make rope, with spools.
- Gold cloth chasuble. The cross is embroidered with gold and the decoration is needle work in China silk.
- The benediction veil dates from the early XVIIIth century and is made of Brussels lace.
- The crinoline skirt of Brussels lace is said to have belonged to the Empress Eugénie in 1867. It is made with spindles and decoration with needlework.
- A miniature banner, of gold lace, made by Miss Ver Elst, depicts the city as it was 1000 years ago.

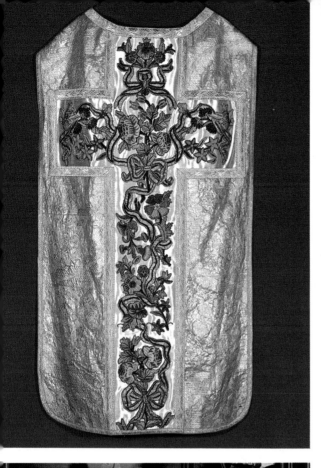

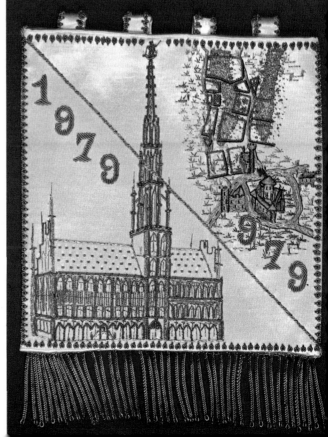

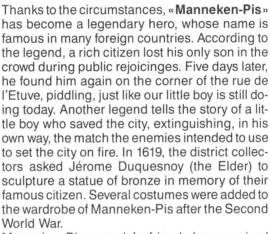

Thanks to the circumstances, «**Manneken-Pis**» has become a legendary hero, whose name is famous in many foreign countries. According to the legend, a rich citizen lost his only son in the crowd during public rejoicinges. Five days later, he found him again on the corner of the rue de l'Etuve, piddling, just like our little boy is still doing today. Another legend tells the story of a little boy who saved the city, extinguishing, in his own way, the match the enemies intended to use to set the city on fire. In 1619, the district collectors asked Jérome Duquesnoy (the Elder) to sculpture a statue of bronze in memory of their famous citizen. Several costumes were added to the wardrobe of Manneken-Pis after the Second World War.

Manneken-Pis, people's friend, has received many military and civil honours and distinctions. On May 1; 1698, the Elector of Bavaria, Maximilian Emmanuel, General Governor of the Netherlands, gave him his first costume. Since then, Lords and Burgesses have offered him the most beautiful clothes. His wardrobe is probably the most complete and varied that has ever existed. It grew very quickly, especially after the First World War. Nowadays, it contains more than 250 costumes, especially aristocratic, military, folklore, carnival costumes and many craft costumes.

The church of «**Notre-Dame de Bon Secours**» was built in Baroque style in 1664 by the architect Jean Cortvriendt. It is topped by an hexagonal cupola. Inside, you can admire three hemispherical apses and galleries. The fonts are decorated with angels'heads made of white marble. The statue of «Notre-Dame de Bon Secours» dates from the XIVth century. It is an isolated, humble but, very pleasant church.

The «**Bourse**» is the meeting-place of the Belgian financial world. It was created by the decree of Juli 8, 1801. It was declared a meeting room by the government, but in 1860, the idea of putting up a building to add to the grandeur of our capital. The foundation stone was laid in 1871. It was built from the plans of the architect Suys, in a Neo-classical style, and was inaugurated on December 27, 1873. The six colums with Corinthian capital are topped by a pediment decorated with a bas-relief representing, « Belgium protecting industry and trade ». The main room is cross-shaped, it is 43 meters long and 37 meters wide and has a cupola supported on 28 colums.

The **Saint Nicolas Church** is dedicated to the patron Saint of merchants. It dates back the origins of the city and is closely related to its history. In the XIth and XIIth centuries, a little river ran around the nave of the church to flow into the Senne near to the Bourse. During the French bombardment in 1695, it was almost totally destroyed. In 1714 it was rebuilt; but again it was destroyed. In 1799, it was parcelled out and sold, but a group of parishioners managed to buy it back, and it was restored to worship in 1804. Many people were in favor of pulling the church down to ease the flow of vehicular and pedestrian traffic. But, in 1954, the officials approved the restoration plans. And it was not long before the edifice looked completely new.

The choir of the church dates from 1381 and the chapel of the Virgin from 1480. The Saint Nicolas church is furnished in Louis IX style. The medaillons of the stalls depict the story of Saint Nicolas, and were made by Van der Haeghen. The choir is closed by a beautiful gate (XVIIIth century). The high altar is decorated with a painting by Helman representing «Jesus curing the Canaanitish woman». The church contains other beautiful altars and a painting by P.P. Rubens «The Virgin and the Sleeping Child».

The **Place de Brouckère** bears the name of the Burgomaster who governed the city from 1848 to 1860. The square is the center of the city. The boulevards which cross it connect the North and South stations. From South to North, they are Boulevard Lemonnier, Boulevard Anspach and Boulevard Adolph Max.

Saint Catherine's church was built in 1854 on the site of the original church by the architect Poelaert. This not very well proportioned church was built in a mixture Norman, Gothic and Renaissance style. The high altar houses a painting depicting «The Assumption of Saint Catherine» by de Craeyer.

The church of «**Saint-Jean Baptiste au Béguinage**» was built between 1657 and 1676. We do not know the name of the architect who built this masterpiece. The façade of the church, plentifully decorated, is said to be one of the most beautiful in Belgium. The inside is wel-proportioned. The rich decoration is illuminated by wide windows. The pulpit evokes Saint Dominique the life of put to death in 1757, from the designs of Smeyers. The name of the church comes from the Grand Béguinage, founded in Brussels in 1250 and destroyed during the French Revolution. It included a dozen little streets.

The new **Church of Finistère** was built between 1708 and 1730. In 1855, the statue of the Virgin; sculpted by Van Arendonck, was placed in the large oblong panel of the façade. The inside consists of three naves. The altars were made of white marble by A.J. Leclercq in 1853. The paneling of the stalls is in Louis XIV style. The choir is surmounted by a hemispherical apse, ornamented with four pilasters with composite capital. The chapel on the right side is decorated by a painting done in 1859 by Severdonck and representing «The Flight to Egypt». The miraculous statue of Our Lady of Finistère is worshipped in this church.

The **Théâtre Royal de la Monnaie** stands in the center of the city. Its name comes from the former Mint in front of it. The present theatre, work of the architect Damesme, was inaugurated on May 25, 1819 by a performance of one of the master-pieces by Grétry, « La Caravane du Caire ». The edifice is of Neo-classical style and is topped by a triangular pediment. In 1851, the city asked the sculptor Eugène Simonis to compose a bas-relief representing « l'Harmonie des Passions Humaines ». The theatre is famous all over the world and can compare with the finest theatres overseas. The performances of M. Béjart and his Ballet of the XXthe century are remarkable. The first episode of the revolution broke out on August 25, 1830, during a performance of « La Muette de Portici ».

The «**Ilot Sacré**» district is situated near the Galleries and the Market Place. The navrow streets are as brisk in daytime as in the evening, and are well-known for their cateres and restaurants of all kinds and all nationalities.

The foundation stone of the **«Galeries Saint-Hubert»** was laid on May 6, 1846, by King Leopod I. The galleries constitue a large passage 212 meters long, 8 meters wide and 18 meters high, and are the work of Cluysenaer. The busts and statues decorating them were created by the sculptor Jacquet. The «Galeries Saint-Hubert» were the first galleries in Europe with shops, restaurants and theatres. Thet are extremely busy.

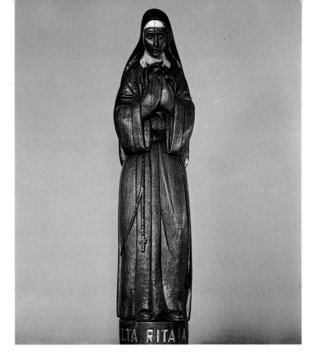

The church of «**La Madeleine**» (XVth century) possesses a bell-turret from the late the XVIIIth century, extremely elegant and well-proportioned. A chapel was added during the restoration of the church in 1957. The origin of the new construction is the façade of Saint Ann's Chapel, erected in 1665 and pulled down in 1927. The Chapel is dedicated to Saint Rita and is decorated with Blank's fresco's.

«**Place de l'Albertine**», where the equestrian statue of Albert I, sculpted by Courtens, stands, opens on to the «Mont des Arts».
The «**The Mont des Arts**» was designed during the reign of Leopold I, construction began when Leopold II was on the throne, and it was finished in the reign of Baudouin I. It is dedicated to Albert I.

Beautiful gardens can be admired on the «**Mont des Arts**». The «Mont des Arts» is surrounded by: the National Library of the «Albertine» which contains more than one million books and about 30,000 manuscripts; the «Palais des Congrès» and the «Palais de la Dynastie» where one can admire a carillon and a clock with an animated dial.

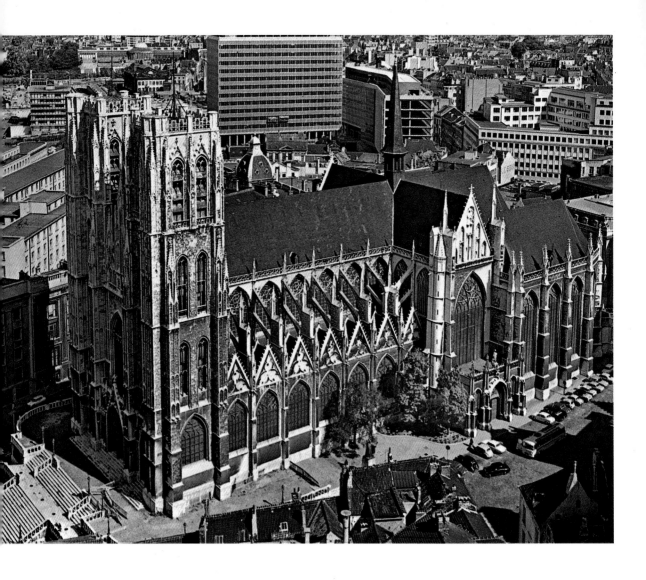

The origin of the « **Cathédrale Saint-Michel** » dates back to the XIIIth century and shows in the plenitude of its greatness and its power the religious art which was the grandeur of the Middle Ages. In 1226 Duke Henri I of Brabant laid the foundation stone of this building, which was only finished under Charles V. This explains the superposition of different styles: Roman-Gothic, Primary, Secondary and Tertiary Gothic, and Renaissance. The main façade, which is founted by a monumental staircase, is comprised of two square towers 69 meters high, which are connected by a gable-end decorated with blind arches and niches. These niches are surmounted by a Saint Michel downing the dragon, and underneath, one can see Saint Gudule between two Saints. There is a great portal in the center, which is decorated with statues of Saints and with historical associations of Brabant. It is surmounted by a huge gothic window. The side walls are also very beautiful from the architectural viewpoint.

The decoration of the temple really enhances its true greatness. The inside is 110 meters long, 50 meters wide and 26 meters high. The Roman columns supporting the arch are decorated with statues of the twelve apostles, sculpted by Duquesnoy, Faid'herbe, Van Mildert and Tobias. The choir is in Primary Gothic style, lit by two huge stained glass windows of the XVIth century. The very luxurious high altar of sculpted cakwood is decorated with symbolic representations made of embossed copper. The pulpit is remarkable. It is the work of H. Verbruggen and belonged to the Jesuits of Louvain who, in 1776, gave it to the collegial church. The wooden sculptures represent Adam and Eve banished from paradise.

The «**Chapelle de Notre-Dame**» (Our lady's Chapel) has stained glass windows completed in 1656 by Jean de la Baer from designs by T. Van Thulden. They represent episodes of Our Lady's life, with the portraits of the people who offered them. In the Chaptel, there is a black and white marble altar of Jean Voorspoel, court architect and apprentice to J. Duquesnoy. It is considered to be one of the most beautiful baroque retables of 1657. The painting representing «the Assumption of the Blessed Virgin» was painted by J.B. Champaigne (1631-1681).

The «**Chapelle du Saint-Sacrement**» (Chapel of the Blessed Sacrament) was built between 1534 and 1539 by Pierre van Wygenhoven. Several stained glass windows depict episodes from the story of the Blessed Sacrament; these are gifts from Charles V's family. Before the altar, a white marble flagstone marks the spot where Archduke Albert and Archduchess Isabelle, who died in 1621 and 1633 respectively, are buried. The retable of the Blessed Sacrament is made of sculpted oak in the Gothic style, and is the work of the Goyers brothers.

The stained glass windows must particulary be appreciated for the richness of harmonious colours and the delicacy of working. Charles V and his wife Isabelle of Portugal adoring the relics of the Blessed Sacrament, it was given by the emperor, from designs by Van Orley (1537).

Louis II and Mary of Hungary, sister of Charles V, kneel before the Holy Trinity. The stained glass window was offered by Mary of Hungary in memory of her husband who died at the age of twenty in battle against the Turks.

The «**Colonne du Congrès**» (Column of the Congress) by J. Poelaert was erected in honor of the National Congress, which wrote the constitution of 1831. The foundation stone was laid on September 25, 1850 by King Leopold I, whose statue tops the 49 meter column. The two bronze lions on the entrance and the bas-reliefs on the pedestral were made by Simonis and symbolize the 9 provinces. The four statues in the corners represent the freedom of the press, the freedom of education, the freedom of association and the freedom of worship.

On November II, 1922, mortal remains of the unknown soldier were buried before the monument between the two lions.

The construction of the «**Palais des Etats Généraux**» started in 1779 from Guimard's plan. The façade was sculpted by Godecharle in 1781. After 1830, it became the «Palais des Nations» including the «Chamber of Deputies» and the «Senate» whose meeting from is decorated with paintings by Gallait and Lalaing.

The **Royal Escort** is composed of the elite corps of the gendarmerie. According to the tradition of gendarmes uniformes before 1314, the pageantry accompanies the King and the Queen during their official ceremonies, Heads of State during their official visits to Belgium, or ambassadors when presenting their credentials to the King.

The Royal Palace is the most imposing monument of this district. The palace originally consisted of two buildings. In 1783 the Abbey of Villers had a hotel built. In 1784, it was sold to the Austrian Governor. Later another hotel was built and declared the residence of the general commander of the Austrian troops. After the Netherlands were created, the building became the residence of King William. The king conceived the idea of joining the two hotels, and entrusted the architect Van der Straeten with the plans, but it was Tielman who concretized his idea in 1827-1829. The palace was modified in 1904 by King Leopold II who had the façade rebuilt in Louis XIV style. The façade is decorated with a bas-relief by T. Vinçotte, which represents Belgium, the Belgian flag in one hand. Belgium is seated between agriculture and industry. Nowadays, it is the official residence of the Belgian sovereigns.

The «**Parc de Bruxelles**» is situated between the Royal Palace and the «Palais des Nations». It is quadrilateral in form and measures 450x320 meters. It was designed by an Austrian architect Zinner, and a French architect Guimard. It stands on the former Warande which was the game reserve of the Duke of Brabant. In the parc, there are two little ornamental pools and beautifully laid-out perspectives. Sculptures of the XVIIIth century have also been erected, but some of there have been replaced by copies. The «Musée des Beaux-Arts» (Fine Arts Museum) possesses the originals. In summer, in the afternoon, music lovers can listen the concerts.

The equestrian statue of Godefroid de Bouillon, first King of Jerusalem, can be seen in the center of the «Place Royal». It was erected in 1848 and is one of the finest works of Eugène Simonis. The hero is represented leaving for the crusades: he is waving the flag and crying «Dieu le veut» (God wills it).

The « **Place Royale** » (Royal Square) was built in the XVIIIth century according to the symetrical plan of Barré and Guimard, and glorifies the reign of Charles of Lorraine.

The Palace of the Dukes of Brabant was several times enlarged under Philip the Good. Charles V abdicated in the great hall of the palace in 1555.

The **Church of Saint-Jacques sur Coudenberg** was built to the plans of Guimard, between 1776 and 1787. The pediment is decorated with a fresco of J. Portaels. The inside shows great simplicity. The allegorical figures of the Old and the New Testament designed by Godecharle decorate the high altar, which is surmounted by tree bas-reliefs by Olivier, representing the Birth of Jesus, the Last Supper and Christ entombed.

The «**Musées Royaux des Beaux-Arts**» (Royal Museums of Fine Arts) of Brussels (paintings and sculptures) are housed in a building of Neo-classical style, built by Balat between 1875 and 1885. The façade of bleu stone has 4 Corinthian columns topped by bronze statues representing painting, sculpture, architecture and music. Above the doors, there are busts of P.P. Rubens, Jean de Bologne and Van Ruysbroeck. At the extremities of the building, two bronze groups right « La glorification de l'art » (the Glorification of art) by P. de Vigne and left « L'Inspiration de l'art » (the Inspiration of Art) by Van der Stappen. They complete the 64 meters long and 18 meters high façade.

A. Van Dyck (1599-1641):
«Rest during the Flight to Egypt».

P.P. Rubens (1577-140):
«The Prodigal Son».

P. Breughel (15-1569): «Winter Landscape».

P. Breughel (1520-1569): «Wedding Feast».

David Teniers (1610-1690): «Flemish Fair».   David Teniers (1610-1690): «The Village Doctor».

On july 20, 1890, the Burgomaster Charles Buls inaugurated the «**Square du Petit Sablon**», which is the work of architect Henri Beyaert. The square is enclosed by a superb balustrade of hand wrought-iron with several motifs. 48 little Gothic columns have been erected at intervals. They are all different and are topped by small stylized bronze statues, symbolizing the crafts of Brussels. In the center of the square stands the statue of the patriot and martyr **Earl of Egmont and Earl of Horn,** who were condemned by the duke of Alba, and beheaded on the Market Place on June 5, 1568. Ten other statues surround this statue. They glorify the people who, thanks to their political action and their genius, characterized the XVIth century in Belgium.

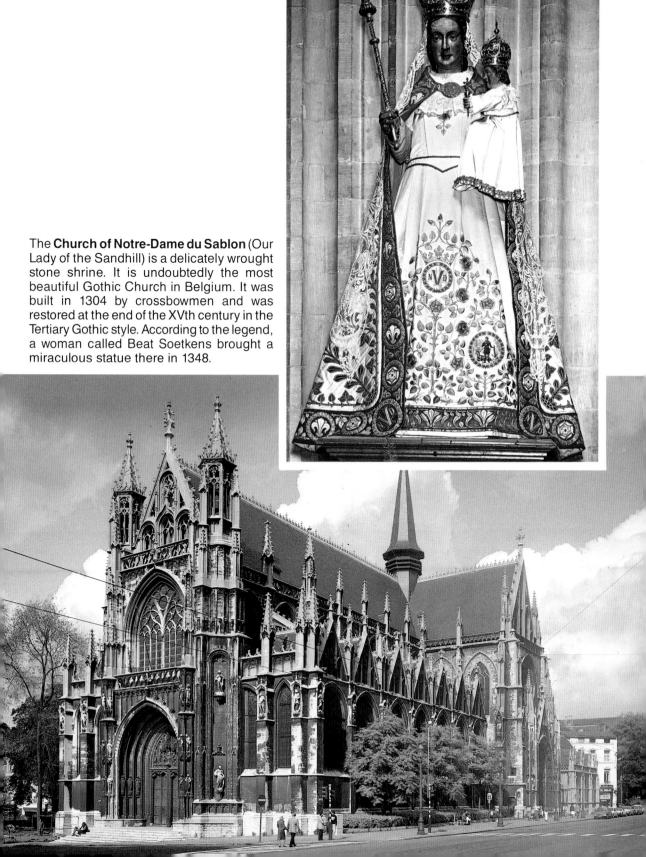

The **Church of Notre-Dame du Sablon** (Our Lady of the Sandhill) is a delicately wrought stone shrine. It is undoubtedly the most beautiful Gothic Church in Belgium. It was built in 1304 by crossbowmen and was restored at the end of the XVth century in the Tertiary Gothic style. According to the legend, a woman called Beat Soetkens brought a miraculous statue there in 1348.

In 1549 the **Sacrarium** was added to the choir. It is a little chapel which serves to preserve the Holy Sacrament. The Chapel of Tour and Tassis was added in 1651 in honor of the Italian familiy which founded in Brussels, during the XVth century, the international postal service.

The surroundings of the «**Place du Sablon**» became during the XVIIth century the very aristocratic district of the city. Manorial houses were erected there. These are depicted in the paintings of Sallaert and remind us of happier times. In the center of the square, wa can admire an impressive fountain sculpted by Jacques Bergé. It is made of white marble and represents Minerve seated. It was a gift of Lord Bruce, Earl of Ailsbury, to thank Brussels for its hospitality during his exile. He died on December 16, 1741, in one of the houses on the Place du Sablon. Today, the Place du Sablon is full of antique shops.

The «**Palais de Justice**» is the most extraordinary monument in Europe. Its total area is about 26,000 square meters. The stairs lead to a bronze door, created by the architect Van Mansfield, giving entry to the waiting hall which is 3,600 square meters. In the whole building, there are 20 hearing rooms, 245 rooms, appartements, cells... The vast hall of the Assize Court was embellished by Delville. The dome is 103 meters above the square and is the work of the architect Benoit. At the four corners of the monument stand 4 statues symbolizing justice, clemency, power and law. The work of the architect Poelaert, started in 1866 and inaugurated on October 15, 1883, aroused a great deal of criticism but is much admired today.

The **Church of Notre-Dame de la Chapelle** was created in 1134 by the Duke of Brabant Godefroid le Barbu, and is one of the most interesting churches in Brussels for its architecture and also for what it reminds us of. It is full of characteristics of Brabançon art: large pilasters, capitals, and columns between the chapels. Huge columns run along the immense nave. The columns constitute a capital on top of which stand the statues of ten of the apostels by Duquesnoy, Faid'herbe, Van Delen and Cosyns, and two statues of Our Lady. The pulpit dates from 1720, and is the work of Plumier. It depicts «Elie sheltered in a grotto and fed by an angel».

Several famous people have their tombs in the church. A white marble epitaph shows that the painter Pieter Breughel was buried in the church in 1569. « Notre Dame de la Solitude » can be worshiped there, it is a Spanish statue brought by the Infanta Isabelle. The stained glass windows are not ancient but very representative:

- The stained glass window of the rood-screen represents « The Assumption of the Virgin » and the « Ascension of Christ » made in 1890 by de Dobbelaere from Bruges.
- « The Bird of the Virgin » and
- « The Presentation of the Virgin » were painted by the artist in stained glass, Van der Poortere in 1862.

The «**Porte de Hal**» (Hal Gates) is the only gate of the second fortification of the town (1357-1383) remaining today. Fortunately, some friends of the «Old Brussels» stepped in to save it from destruction. It was transformed in the years 1868 to 1870, under the guidance of the architect Beyaert. Today, this building has become the «Musée Royal d'Armes et Armures».

The «**Place du Jeu de Balle**» is situated in the center of the popular district of the city. Saturday and Sunday are market days. You can find there recent or ancient objects from old attics. It happens in a very unusual atmosphere. On the corner of the rue Haute and the rue de la Porte Rouge, you can seen the house of Pieter Breughel the Old. His grand-son David Teniers III died there on February 2, 1685. On December 14, 1924, the commemorative tablet with the inscription «Homage of the people to their famous painter» was unveiled.

The headquarters of the Commission and the Council of Ministers of the European Community called « **Common Market** » are in Brussels. The treaty which set up the E.E.C. was signed in Rome on March 25, 1957. At the time three communities were referred to: the ECCS (European Community of Coal and Steel) set up in April 1951, the Euratom concerned with the peaceful use of nuclear power, and the European Economic Community. The three institutions merged in 1967. There are now five institutions: The European Parliament, The Council of Ministers with representatives of all the member states, The Court of Justice whose task it is to ensure the respect of the Law in accordance with the provisions of the Treaties, The Economic and Social Council and the Commission. The Commission is the defender of the Treaties, the executive body of the Community. It also initiates the policies of the Commission whose unity and coherence it must safeguard and is the mounthpiece of the Community in trade negotions.

The «**Palais du Cinquantenaire**» was created at the time of the exhibition of 1880 to commemorate the fiftieth anniversary of Belgian independence. The Palace was built from the plans of G. Bordiau. The central path of the garden leads to the Triumph Arch which is 45 m high and has three archways (one archway is 10 m wide). This monument was built by the French architect G. Girault. The quadriga which dominates the top was sculpted by T. Vinçotte. It symbolizes «Belgium triumphant heading for the future» and was created in 1905, at the time of the 75th anniversary of our independance. The palace consists of two large aisles housing museums.

In the first part, the «**Musée de l'Armée**» (Museum of Army) houses numerous very interesting collections: a library, about 25,000 books, records, memorials of Belgium's struggles, patriotic badges, medals, ... arms, uniforms and flags.

The other part contains the «**Musée Royaux d'Art et d'Histoire**» (Royal Museums of Art and History). The museums are very rich and are amongst the most famous museum in Europe.

They preserve collections of prehistory, Egyptian, Greek, Roman, Asiatic and American antiques, collections of art and ethnography, folklore and oriental art.

King Leopold II had the «**Basilique Nationale du Sacré Coeur**» built: he laid the foundation in 1905. It should have been a building of Neo-gothic style but in 1919, the architect Van Nuffel drew new plans. There where completed in 1970. The central nave measures 165 meters and the transept 108 meters. The towers-65 meters high-and the dome on the top reach a total height of 100 meters. The inside is covered with Terra Cotta and there are splendid stained glass windows.

The «**Grands Palais du Heysel**» were built for the International Exhibition of 1935. They were enlarged several times. Other parts were added for the Universal Exhibition of 1958. The international exhibitions, the Car Show, and the Ideal Home Exhibition are held there. The Central Hall is beautiful, because of its simple, modern style. The concrete arches are 80 meters wide and 31 meters high.

On the occasion of the International Exhibition in 1935 a **Planetarium** was founded on the request of King Albert I and was named «Alberteum». The present planetarium replaces the preceding one and was built between 1970 and 1973. It was officially opened on Septembre 28, 1976.

The Zeiss Planetarium is a complicated apparatus with 119 optical projection systems. It offers a unique and breath-taking scientific sight. The sky with its 6,000 perceptible stars is a thrilling scientific exhibition. The planetarium is established in a room of 25m diameter and has 350 seats.

The Church **"Notre-Dame de Laeken"** is in gothic style. Its construction started in 1854, realizing the plans of the architect Poelaert. In 1908, von Schmidt of Munich added the porch and the spire. It was erected in the memory of the first Belgian Queen. It is the burial-place of the members of the Royal Family.

The «**Castle of Laeken**» was built under the Austrian domination from 1782 to 1784. The plans were drawn by the architect Montoyer. In 1802, the castle became the property of Napoelon I who spent a few days there in 1815. The day after his accession to the throne, King Leopold I took up residence there. It has now become the private residence of the Belgian King and Queen.

In «**The Royal Glass House**» grow very rich collections of exotic plants. They are open to the public for a few days in May.

In front of the castle stands «**The Monument to Leopold I**», first king of the Belgians. It is 50 meters high, and the statue was sculptured by Geets (1880).

The «**Palais du Belvédère**» is a beautiful building. It is in Louis XIV style and has a dome. Viscount Walckiers had it built in 1788 and it was restored in 1957. It is fronted by a marvellous garden and terraces. It is the residence of Their Royal Highnesses Prince Albert and Princess Paola.

The decoration of the «**Pavillon Chinois**» (Chinese Pavilion) are very exotic. Extraordinary collections of China and other Chinese and Japanese art objets of the XVIIth and XVIIIth centuries.

The «**Tour Japonaise**» (Japanese Tower) (80 meters high) and the «Pavillon Chinois» are jewels of Oriental art. They come from the exhibition of Paris (1900) and were rebuilt under the reign of King Leopold II.

Brussels is famous for its beautiful **lace**. You can admire it especially near the Market Place.
- Collar made of fine duchess and needly-point lace.
- Broad-brimmed handkerchief in beautiful needle-point lace, also called «Point de Rose».
- Rectangular cloth (35x45) in authentic hemstitched Brussels lace.

The Royal Museum of Central Africa in Tervuren was built by King Leopold II, who gave it to the nation. It was built from the plans of the architect Girault and inaugurated in 1910 by King Albert. The palace, in Louis XVI style, is surrounded by a park of more than 200 ha. The museum contains a rich collection of objects made by the natives of Zaïre. They give an idea of the country, the live of its inhabitants, the costums and religious rites.

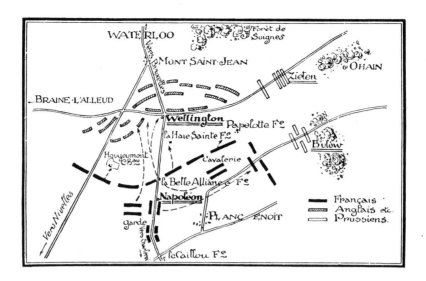

Waterloo is a Commune in Brabant, south of Brussels. It has become famous owing to the battle that took place on its territory. On June 18, 1815, in fact shortly after Napoleon had come back to France, the battle of Waterloo to the Napoleon era. Face to face were 74,000 French soldiers and 67,000 allied soldiers belonging to British and Dutch-Belgian forces under Well-ington's command, along with Blücher's Prussian army. After a day of fierce fighting, the Emperor found himself attacked from both sides. Believing that General Grouchy would arrive, he had allowed himself to be surrounded by Allied Forces. On the battle field 27,000 French soldiers and 22,000 Allied soldiers lost their lives. The battle had only lasted 24 hours.

Duke of Wellington (1769-1852).

Prince William of Orange (1792-1849).

Marshal Blücher (1742-1819).

Wellington and Blücher congratulating each other on their victory.

The lion, symbolizing England and the Netherlands, is the work of the sculptor Van Geel of Mechelen. Made of castiron it is 4.50 long and 4.45 m high and weighs 28 tons. The pedestal which is 6 m high, with it foundations deep in solid ground, bears simply the date of the day when the glory of the great Emperor came to an end. The knoll was erected in 1826 on the spot where the Prince d'Orange was wounded trying to break the attack of the French Guard. The great amount of soil necessary to build this monument was provided by the women of Liège, who carried it in baskets on their backs. 228 steps lead to the top of the conical knoll, which is 40.50 meters high.

INDEX